MW00878534

Anticipating More:

Poetry of the Grand Canyon

Diane Brown Benninghoff

Copyright © 2012 Diane Brown Benninghoff

All rights reserved.

ISBN: 1475196229
ISBN-13: 978-1475196221

Anticipating More

"We have an unknown distance yet to run, an unknown river to explore. What falls there are, we know not; what rocks beset the channel, we know not; what walls ride over the river, we know not. Ah, well! we may conjecture many things."

John Wesley Powell

The Poems

Anticipating More

Time

Spending time…

time laughing,

        quiet or raucous,

        a giggle or a loud guffaw.

time singing,

        songs I never knew,

        yet always knew.

 time knowing,

        about this place,

        about you,

        about myself.

The laughter –

    The singing –

        The lessons learned.

        Now with me for a lifetime,

        a moment.

Layers of miracles –

        one atop another

        forming a record of this time.

The Tree

Reaching up.

Reaching out.

Twisted,

    curved,

        tortured.

Stories to tell

    of floods,

    of drought.

    Of bird,

    lizard,

    and man.

Pruned by the wind.

Dying in stages,

living on hope,

    it shades me today,

giving its all in a hostile world.

Looking Over the Least of Them

Poor little bat shivering on the deck.

What brought him here in the light of day?

       Did his navigating system fail him?

       Has he been riding with us all day?

       Did he fall from the sky?

       Have too much tequila?

Is he dying?

       Should we bury him in a watery grave?

His savior's voice comes –

      He's just cold – give him to me.

      Let him rest, warm up.

      Give him a chance to live.

       Look into his eyes –

          Hope shines there.

The Bat-faced woman is nearby

      looking over the least of them.

The Admiral

Tales to tell.

Trails traveled,

Rapids run.

Battles won –

      And lost.

One of a kind –

A legend –

    (happens if you

        live long enough

        and stick to your guns.)

With a passion for a place and a way of life.

Anger at those

    who destroyed the places he loves

    and are still trying.

        Righteous anger.

Scorn (with a smile?)

    for the god-damn "privates,"

the Park Circus,

all fools.

But now –

over time –

Witness

a kinder, gentler spirit

than the sagas tell.

And the bucket-assed kid

rows on –

rows on –

rows for me.

A gift.

An honor.

A god-damn honor

To be here.

Now.

With the Admiral.

Yahoo.

Tapeats

Even in the bright sun,

    the contours,

    holes,

    ledges of the sandstone

    invite my touch –

    curve in sensuous ways.

Home to the fortunate

    wrens,

    lizards,

    mice,

    and, for now – me.

At night, an almost full moon.

    A magical sight comes alive.

    Shapes change – glow from within.

    Form captures shadows.

        Captures me.

Sweet

Those songs we heard so long ago.

Sweet to hear them here.

As the guitars pick out the parts,

    You pick out the words,

    She picks out the harmony.

Songs,

    Laughter,

        Rhythms of the night,

           Memories of the past –

New memories being made.

The shadows grow,

    The stars come out to play,

        The moon casts its glow.

And melodies of memory remain.

Sweet.

Squirrel Camp

Look up!

It's a squirrel sitting tall,

      paws up,

           gazing up stream.

Transfixed.

Motionless.

The fading light silhouettes

his shape

against the sky,

Move squirrel!

But he does not move –

      he is petrified –

      has become a rock.

See him?

      Look up.

He will Crash into Camp –

this year

or next,

or in a thousand years.

But for now, stands as sentinel.

Watches over us in this rocky spot.

Look up!

Smiles, Laughs, Tears

Tell me a story - a poem - a joke - a song.

A story that makes me wonder, or understand.

    A story of another time or place.

        A story that makes me smile.

A poem that lets me see in new ways –

    comprehend,

        imagine.

            Makes me laugh or weep.

A joke – simple or shaggy,

    fresh or moldy,

        that makes me groan or grin.

Sing me a song.

    A song I know but have never heard,

    and I'll sing along

    when I don't know the words.

Running into Rocks

Toes, knees, ankles, boats

are attracted to rocks.

Some rocks are magnets,

with an attraction little understood.

Ask my shin.

Promises

Promise me –

    you will help the willows return.

Promise me –

    the long march will end

    with a burbling stream.

Promise me –

    the cloud will give a few minutes of shade.

    We will live with eyes open

      to star glitter,

        caressing nights,

          feathery dawns.

    We will need no conversation to share a
moment –

    but can talk about anything.

        That the smooth liquids of the river,

          the rum, the light of the moon

        will become one.

    That you will get my joke when no one else
does – *most* of the time.

Promise me - just promise.

    Even if you lie.

National Secret

Somewhere there's a fire,

    or a dust storm,

    or magic.

But always the drama

    of early morning light –

    of the unknown.

Secrets wait to appear as if out of the mist.

    To be uncovered,

        decoded,

            perhaps, understood.

For most – such places are a National Secret.

The Lizard Gets His Grub

Personally, I love avocados

Piled on the meatcheesetomatopicklelettuce –

    And rings of red onion!

This critter prefers something *else* for lunch.

But always something green!

Maybe he'd like a little wasabi?

Jewels

Pretty little things.

Gems, really.

Sparkling in this sun-soaked day.

Glittering with possibilities.

A gem can make my day.

Make my world look

     new, ancient,

     rough, polished.

          Agate, Sapphire, Turquoise,

          Emerald, Ruby, Serpentine

           All strung together

           To string me out.

From wave of pleasure,

To wave of pleasure.

The gift of jewels –

     Thrills when offered.

     Exacts a price.

Give me gems, and I'm all yours.

15

Jake

Jake – is that you?

Moon is full,

Spirits are around us

 along with the moon-dimmed stars,

  a bat now and then,

   a scurrying critter, night vision working.

         Quiet.

Jake – is that you?

  Wandering still,

  over the flats,

  searching for your tongue?

       You shouldn't have lied.

Find it,

  rest in peace,

become whole,

the after-life awaits.

If only…

Jake – is that you?

I saw your tongue today,

high on that ridge,

waiting for you

up there.

Jake – Jake, is that you?

No sound.

No answer.

He is here.

In the air

Sweat,

clean sweat

on a man –

                                       ambrosia.

Telling of effort.

Sweat honestly

earned in the hot sun.

       There was a time we all knew,

       Craved, this scent –

                               an aphrodisiac

Washed away each day to return

with the rising of the sun and the challenges

of a new day.

I could wrap myself in that perfume

of soap and sweat –

clean sweat –

                                    on a man.

Haiku

Dox

Bring back the Tapeats

Or the Muav's soft forms – but Dox?

A Pox on Dox.

Adults at Play

Splash, giggle and grin.

Sing, shout, just because you can.

Adults are at play.

Dancing in the Dark

Their own mirror ball

Rotates above

With a million shards of light.

The music moves them smoothly,

(Or their movement helps the

river band keep measured time.)

Movements lubricated with whiskey,

    Or love,

    Or history

Make the sandy ballroom floor glide easily.

Watch how they hold one another,

Watch how they move as one.

    Envy.

They've done this before.

They will do this again –

But never in this magic circle of friends.

Surrounded by wonder

At them,

At where we are,

At the nostalgia growing as

The dance, the music,

and the two-week instant

Draws to a close.

A river dance

Locked in memory.

Click

You don't see *this* at home!

Bright, distant, near-enough-to-touch cliffs

cut into a preposterous sky.

      Bathed in light, caught in shadow,

      change in a flash.

Forget the camera.

The best image –

    Clicks in my mind,

    Stays in my memory,

    In the recesses of my heart –

    And endures.

I *will* see this at home.

As it Turns Out

There are days,

    and there are days.

No matter how great the skill or talent –

    Trouble.

Wave trains with a come-hither attraction.

    The "kiss-the-edge" that becomes a French kiss,

        with a deeper involvement than planned.

Menacing boils and whirlpools

    ready to take you in, under.

Endless eddies,

    set on holding you tight.

Rock gardens.

    Just waiting for a fragile craft –

    Wanting just a *small* bite.

Reminders of who, what, is in control.

Changes

I began as one thing –

    but heat, pressure, time

    has had its way with me.

Pushed me into a shape

that fits a new world,

a new reality.

Deep in the labyrinth –

eyes, then thoughts, lift

to imagine a new me.

No escaping the changes.

    Some abrupt.

    Some over time.

I am metamorphosed.

Blooming

Among vertical cliffs

And walls telling stories of the past –

                                A fragile blossom.

In the midst of sand,

Buffeted by wind –

        Fragile,

        Unassuming,

        Sweet,

        Enduring.

                        It dances to its own tune.

I came for the breathtaking sights,

        The grandeur.

        To be awed.

But the little blossom tells me

                        This is why I am here.

Beautiful Women

"All these women are beautiful," he said.

Wise man.

Grown women.

Who know who they are.
    But still look for nuance.
        Still completing themselves.
Always open to the new
        experience,
            challenge,
                opportunity,
                    friendship.
No makeup here –
        Skin glows in the heat of the day.
        Glows differently
        in the light of the stars.

Hair,

Blonddarkgraylongshort –

shining,

fragrant with silty water.

Bodies –

Tall, short, delicate, strong.

Fit for the challenge.

Calves shaped by the climb.

Arms strong enough to hold what must be held.

Eyes

luminous with wonder,

bright with humor,

deep with experience,

steady in their gaze.

Wisdom in those eyes.

No girlish giggles here.

A throaty laugh,

a knowing smile,

a sigh at just the right time.

A "yahoo" now and then.

Women who have known

    other places,

    other times,

    other women – and like them.

    Known men – and like *most* of them.

Women who know/have known

    love, heartbreak, friendship,

       and are open for more.

Perfectly imperfect.

Beautiful.

ACKNOWLEDGMENTS

As always, my thanks to Jane Hilberry who gave
me the courage to write.

To my husband, who first got me on the river and
with whom I have kayaked and rafted the great rivers
of the West.

To Matt Herrman, and the crews of Moki Mac who
have taken so many groups of Colorado College
alumni and parents through the Grand Canyon.
And to those fellow boaters – whose words are here.

And to Colorado College, for making it possible for so
many members of the CC family to experience the
wonder of it all.

ABOUT THE AUTHOR

Diane Benninghoff has loved rivers and the places
they have taken her for decades. From her first trips as a
novice kayaker in the early 1970's and through all those
years of kayaking and rafting in her own boats with her
husband and friends, she has tried to share that love
with everyone she knows.

Working with alumni and parents at Colorado
College gave her the opportunity to organize trips on the
Yampa, the Middle Fork of the Salmon, and most
frequently, the Colorado River through Grand Canyon.

This is the author's third chapbook of poems.

Made in United States
Orlando, FL
22 April 2024

46069434R00024